M000226481

The Little
Book of
Reiki

To Katya and Kevin B
(an unlikely pairing!),
with all my love.

The Little
Book of
Reiki

Una L. Tudor

GAIA

First published in Great Britain in 2021 by Gaia, an imprint of
Octopus Publishing Group Ltd
Carmelite House
50 Victoria Embankment
London EC4Y 0DZ
www.octopusbooks.co.uk

An Hachette UK Company
www.hachette.co.uk

Distributed in the US by
Hachette Book Group
1290 Avenue of the Americas
4th and 5th Floors
New York, NY 10104

Distributed in Canada by
Canadian Manda Group
664 Annette St.
Toronto, Ontario, Canada M6S 2C8

ISBN 978-1-85675-444-6

A CIP catalogue record for this book is available
from the British Library.

Printed and bound in China

10 9 8 7 6 5 4 3 2 1

Commissioning Editor: Natalie Bradley
Senior Editor: Faye Robson
Copyeditor: Jane Birch
Art Director: Juliette Norsworthy
Design and illustrations: Abi Read
Production Controller: Serena Savini

Contents

Introduction

The Power of Energy

Reiki:

Mysterious atmosphere

Miraculous sign

Universal energy

This book will not teach you to become a reiki practitioner.

It will not enable you to cure people with a simple laying-on of hands or to run reiki classes or energy workshops. This book will not make you magic or give you special powers. This book will give you, in fact, nothing that you don't already have.

But here's the thing: you already have everything you need, right where you need it. You already have everything that you're hoping this book will give you. You are enough, right now. You are good enough, brave enough, determined enough to be the person you want to be. You just need a little help accessing it. This book is that help.

This book is that *miraculous sign* you've been waiting for: this is it. From now, you're going to be the person you want to be; you're going to understand yourself, and you're going to understand other people; you're going to set out to achieve what you really want to achieve, and you're going to achieve whatever you set out to do.

You're good enough.

You can do this.

We can do this.

What is Reiki?

Reiki is, put simply, a system of healing. It relies on the laying-on of hands – or, in some cases, the *almost* laying-on of hands – to move energy around the physical body. My energy moves yours; your energy moves mine. Like a pair of magnets, we are intrinsically connected through forces beyond our understanding, and these forces drive us. This movement of energy keeps us happy and healthy. Reiki is often called 'spiritual healing', or 'energetic healing';

it is actually often seen as a little controversial, and brushed away as 'New Age' or 'pseudoscience'. You might even feel a little sceptical yourself, and you know what? That's fine. It is *fine* to feel your feelings here. We have room for you; room for your scepticism, for your doubts, for your fears. You are a whole person – a smart, thoughtful person! – and maybe you're not sure. But, nonetheless, you've picked up this book.

And you've picked up this book because something is *wrong*. You've tried more conventional paths, and they haven't worked for you. Something in you wants to learn to make things better. Something in you is crying out to be healed in some way, and there's a part of you that really hopes this book might be the thing that does it.

And I think it might be, too.

This is not a reiki textbook: we won't be making any outsized claims about the science of reiki. Unlike many reiki practitioners, I'm not very interested in telling a fairy story about where reiki comes from; unlike many scholars, I'm not at all interested in trying to debunk something that brings comfort, joy and healing to millions. I am interested, simply, in wellbeing: yours and mine. Ours.

A Science and an Art

Reiki is both a science and an art, and while it's possible for anyone to learn it, you need a master to officially show you the way: you need someone to open the door for you. It is a controlled subject that must be communicated in a reiki workshop: each class gives us a new level of 'attunement' – bringing us into a kind of cosmic harmony – that allows us to practise reiki as masters. Each attunement is a version of the revelations experienced by Mikao Usui (or 'Usui Sensei', as he is respectfully known) – the founder of reiki as we

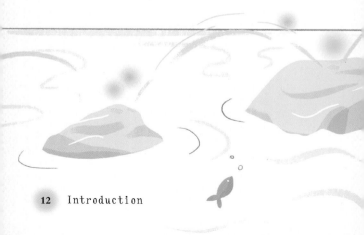

know it and the man who brought reiki to the mainstream – and is powerful in its own right. We learn different principles at each stage of attunement, and only after Stage Three are we able to practise reiki on others. Some things, like the reiki symbols, are so sacred they can traditionally only be communicated in these classes. And so, while anyone can become a reiki master (really!), it would be unethical and against the spirit of reiki for me to suggest this book would give you that power.

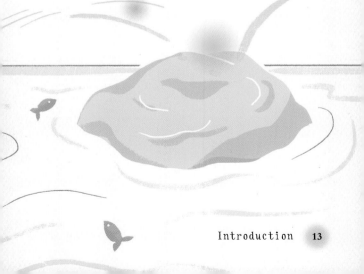

How Can This Book Help?

And yet there are reasons I think this book will help you. There are reasons I think reiki has a phenomenal power to heal, to help, to bring us closer to a kind of *wholeness* that lets us be the person we know is within us. Reiki is about connection, about handing down knowledge from master to student, about passing along *universal energy* from person to person, soul to soul. It's about a human connection, and that's what this book is: it's a connection between me and you; a connection and a collaboration.

Together, we'll learn the basic tenets of reiki; we'll learn what it is, and how it works, and then we'll take those lessons — that *mysterious atmosphere* — and learn how to apply them to our own lives. We're going to see what makes reiki work, and then make it work for us. We're going to open our own doors, and find, I hope, our own paths to healing.

If we're lucky, we might even find out why we hurt in the first place.

Five Precepts

Reiki is therapy; it's communion; it's communication. It's intention and connection; a question and solution; a kind of internal revolution. It's about taking charge of the energy that forms us and drives us forward; it's about healing and wholeness. It's about hope.

There's one more thing, before we begin. You learn these, usually, on a reiki Stage One course, but there's something so important, so universal and so necessary about these that I want us to look at them right now. I want us to carry these with us through every choice we make; every word we read; through every moment we live from now on.

Usui Sensei laid down Five Precepts for reiki practitioners. And I think they work for everyone, whether you're into reiki or not.

Five Precepts for a happy life, five statements to live by.

Just for today...

Do not get angry

Do not worry

Work hard

Be grateful

Be kind

1

Question

The Power of Touch

Touch is Communication

The first sense we acquire is touch.

Deep in the dark of the womb, our senses and systems respond to the lightest of touches and the smallest of movements. It has been said that a foetus of eight weeks old will move instinctively away from the gentle caress of a single hair, which shouldn't really surprise us. Even an amoeba, microscopically small, lacking both brain and nervous system, can detect movement. Touch is the earliest and most basic of all the ways in which we can interact with the world around us and remains, as we develop and change, one of the most crucial. It is highly nuanced and profoundly sophisticated – rich, deep and immensely powerful.

In some ways it might even be argued that touch – if we can define touch as *one thing against another* – is at the heart of all the other senses: the molecules of a blooming flower brushing against the olfactory cells of the nose, the particles of sea salt against the taste buds of the tongue, even sight itself depends on the movement of reflected light coming up against the retina and so into the photoreceptors of the eye, and the brain. These forms of touch are more complex, and yet touch they are still. Touch is the means by which we interact with the world. It is the means by which we interact with everything that exists, and ever will exist. Touch, in short, is shorthand for connection; touch is communication.

The Five Senses

This is a tiny little exercise, based, as so many of these exercises are, in mindfulness practice.

Sit comfortably, any way you like, and take a few deep breaths. Notice your breathing: in and out, in and out. You don't have to change it, just like you don't have to change yourself. Your breath has got you this far, hasn't it? It will keep going, and so will you. Breathe in, breathe out. Close your eyes, if you feel comfortable doing that.

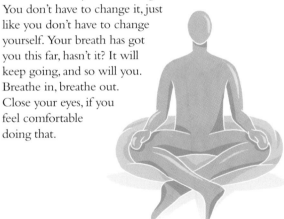

Now, put simply, I want you to notice things.

I want you to notice everything you are touching, right now. Write them down, if you feel like it. Every single thing. Start with your hands: this book! How does this book feel? Concentrate on the sensations, like you've never felt anything before. Are you sitting down? Are there cushions or slats on the back of the chair? Are your feet on the ground or on the coffee table? What sensations can you feel? How can you feel them? What sensations of touch are you experiencing?

What do those sensations evoke for you? Comfort? Stress? Pain? Memories? Really think about it.

The Power of Touch

To understand touch and its true power, we need to travel back more than 50 years, to the mid-20th century: to 1950s America and the psychological research lab – and monkey colony – of one Harry Harlow. Harlow, a National Medal of Science winner, was the President of the American Psychological Association. Even now, he remains one of the most cited (and controversial) figures in psychiatry.

Unusually, however, the controversy surrounding Harlow is not to do with his results, but his methods. Indeed, it is difficult to read the details of his experiments without flinching. Rightly, Harlow's work is now regarded as deeply unethical, but his conclusions remain both moving and crucial to our understanding of human existence.

Harlow, who had established a colony of macaque monkeys, began to study 'attachment'. He did this by taking most of the baby monkeys from their mothers (leaving a control group), and dividing them into groups. To some of the baby monkeys he gave 'cloth mothers', to others 'wire mothers' and to others still, no mothers at all. The cloth mothers were soft and tactile; the wire mothers simply bare frames for holding milk. All the baby monkeys were given everything necessary for their survival. And yet, of course, the monkeys without mothers refused to thrive. The monkeys with only wire mothers refused to thrive. The monkeys with cloth mothers did better, but not nearly so well as the monkeys left with their real mothers.

Furthermore, when given the choice between a wire mother with milk or a cloth mother without milk, the babies chose to cling to the cloth mother each time. The power of touch overwhelmed all other needs.

What other scientists called 'attachment', Harlow called 'love', and when we consider the study proper, we see what we're really talking about here is touch. We are looking at touch as connection, touch as attachment and touch as love.

We Need Touch

Of course, the results of Harlow's experiments seem obvious to us today. We, generations on, now understand intellectually what the earliest humans knew instinctively: babies need to be held, and babies need to be touched. And yet these results were necessary. For previous generations had been told, over and over again, that to touch a child was to harm them. To cuddle your baby was to spoil her, to soften her, to – in the words of one renowned child psychologist – 'inflict a never-healing wound...which may wreck your adult son or daughter's vocational future and their chances for marital happiness'. John B Watson, author of the widely read 1928 book *Psychological Care of Infant and Child*, summed up the attitudes of a century: touching your child is dangerous, powerful and must be rationed. 'Give them a pat on the head if they have made an extraordinarily good job of a difficult task,' Watson wrote, grudgingly, adding later: 'if you must.' It is into this world that Harlow's results come, and into this world that they are so needed.

Without touch, even when provided with everything else they needed, the baby monkeys became not only afraid, but physically weaker. They were notably less healthy, they failed to digest their food properly, they were prone to stomach upsets and sickness. The mental stress arising from the lack

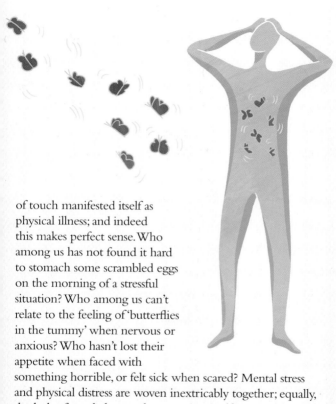

of touch manifested itself as physical illness; and indeed this makes perfect sense. Who among us has not found it hard to stomach some scrambled eggs on the morning of a stressful situation? Who among us can't relate to the feeling of 'butterflies in the tummy' when nervous or anxious? Who hasn't lost their appetite when faced with something horrible, or felt sick when scared? Mental stress and physical distress are woven inextricably together; equally, the lack of touch, love and connection itself can *cause* mental stress, and thus physical distress.

We are physical beings who exist in the world, and every intangible feeling has a tangible form. Our feelings of sadness produce physical tears, which are chemically different to tears from, say, cutting onions. Our feelings of love for a newborn baby, say, or a new sexual partner produce oxytocin, a hormone that has scientifically been shown to reduce physical stress. For every action there is, as Isaac Newton explained, an equal and opposite reaction: our bodies and minds are one.

It is, then, both scientifically proven and intuitively obvious that we do not and cannot exist in a vacuum. The mind cannot exist without the body, the body without the mind, and neither can thrive without the touch and support and love of others.

Everything is Energy

We are made of atoms that shift and move. Of all the atoms that make up you, 98 per cent will be replaced by this time next year. A 1953 study published in the Annual Report for the Smithsonian Institution (as reported by American media organization National Public Radio) revealed that we are shifting, changing creatures, constantly absorbing energy from the world around us. And the world around us is shifting, too: the 'father of quantum physics', Max Planck, wrote a hundred years ago of the ways the universe seemed to him to be made up of moving, changing energies. We now know this to be scientifically true on many levels.

This is energy; energy is 'ki'; 'ki', as in 'qui', as in 'chi', as in 'rei ki': life force.

Everything is energy, and everything is changing: everything is capable of change.

The Ship of Theseus

Long ago, in Ancient Greece, there was a famous sailor named Theseus. He sailed for many years in a magnificent ship, and over the years – as ships do, as everything does – the ship began to need repair. A rotten plank replaced here, a patch on the sail there. New varnish. Gradually, over many years, the ship had been mended so much that not a single particle of the original ship remained. Is that repaired ship still the ship of Theseus?

Now, what if each particle of the old ship – every splinter, every thread – by some miracle washed up on a desert island, and by some miracle the inhabitants of this island built from these particles a perfect replica of the ship itself, each splinter and thread restored to its original place? Would that ship, that island ship, be the ship of Theseus, too?

This is an ancient puzzle, and one that comes in many forms: sometimes the ship of Theseus is being preserved in a museum and gently restored for thousands of years; sometimes, instead of a ship, the subject of the puzzle is a bed or a flowing river. Yet the central question remains the same: what are we, if everything we are is replaced? What makes us the same? What makes us different? What holds us together?

We are a holistic system, made up of all these changing parts. We change, we learn, we learn from others, and so our actions become manifestations of the actions of those we have learned from, and so our thoughts are shaped by the thoughts of those who came before. In Zen Buddhism, we talk often of the transmission of thoughts, and therefore actions, down from the Buddha himself, from teacher to teacher; thus the Buddha actively has a hand in changing the world we live in. There is no self, according to Zen Buddhism, only chains of interlinked energy, absorbing and influencing each other.

The idea of connection, more than anything, can help us understand reiki.

2

Action

The Power of Pain

If it feels like it has taken us a little while to come back to reiki itself, that is because the system of reiki, as properly practised, is a system that needs you to understand the way the world works. We need to understand ourselves as shifting, changing bundles of energy, influenced and influencing, before we can possibly begin to learn how to take control of those influences with intention and purpose.

More than that, we need to let ourselves understand how wide-ranging the subject of energetic healing can be. While reiki itself dates back only a hundred years, every culture through history has understood – in its own way – the subjects we touch on here. Science and spiritualism are in agreement. Matter is energy; energy is intrinsic to all life; energy can neither be created nor destroyed.

Putting Aside the Past

Why does this understanding of energy matter? It matters because let's call this a place to leave any scepticism at the door: let's call this a place to put down any baggage we're carrying before we begin. Let's call this a kind of checkpoint. Nobody comes to a book like this without some kind of trauma, without hopes and fears and ideas that might hold us back. We are here because we think something in this system of touch – of touch, energy and loving care – might help us, but there are probably things already in the way.

So before we can begin, we need to find a safe way to get through those blockages. We need to find somewhere safe to put our past down. We need to ask ourselves the big questions before we can start to find answers.

Let's start with a breathing exercise, drawn from Zen meditation but used more often now in mindfulness classes. It's called a body scan, and it's a good way to allow ourselves the space to ask: *what hurts?*

What hurts? Do I hurt? Is this okay, and is this good, and what do I hope to heal?

Full Body Scan

Sit comfortably, any way you like, and take a few deep breaths. Notice your breathing: in and out, in and out. You don't have to change it, just like you don't have to change yourself. Your breath has got you this far, hasn't it? Breathe in, breathe out. Close your eyes, if you feel comfortable doing that. (You remember this bit from the Five Senses exercise on page 21.)

Now, we're going to notice everywhere we can feel pressure: clothes? The chair? The floor or bed? Is anything digging in or hurting? Can we change anything? Change position now, if you need to. This is permission to find a way of being that is comfortable and natural; to adjust a waistband, to stretch, to move before we settle into stillness together.

Consider, too, your mind: how do you feel taking this much notice of your own processes and your own body? Do you feel self-indulgent, or does it feel nice to finally acknowledge yourself as a being? Does anything hurt? Do you hurt? Acknowledge your body; acknowledge your breath; acknowledge your thoughts. It doesn't matter if your thoughts are wandering; simply nod hello to each thought, accept it and put it to one side for later. It's okay.

Let's come back, then, to our breath. We're going to use our ordinary breath as a kind of thread to follow: a rhythm to run through our body, the way it's run through the body since the earliest moment of our existence as a person in the world. Trust the breath; trust yourself. Consider the breath carefully, as if each one were again that first breath, that earliest moment of self-sustenance. Notice the way your breath feels in your body. Do your shoulders rise? Does your tummy fall? How does it change how you sit against the bed or chair? How does it change how you interact with your environment? Follow the breath in, and out. In, and out.

Taste the breath. Understand that as you draw the air in, you change it; it is altered by the contact it has with you. You change the world every time you breathe.

Bring this awareness to your feet: not just your feet, but your little toes. Can you feel them? Do they touch anything? Does anything touch them? Consider the toes; breathe down right into your toes. Do they hurt? Does anything hurt? Do you hurt? Is this okay?

Bring the attention now into the next toe, then the next, then the next and the next; then the soles of your feet, the tops of your feet, your Achilles tendons, ankles and calves. Do they hurt? Does anything hurt?

Bring this focus – this care – up through your body, like a physio would for a player after a hard match. Notice anything – any old aches, any discomfort, any pain you've been carrying for so long you've stopped acknowledging it. Your thighs, hips, pelvis, sitting bones, stomach. Is that good? Consider your back carefully: so many of us carry tension there. Acknowledge it, and direct the breath to it, in whatever way best works for you.

Do you hurt? Where do you hurt? Bring your attention into your arms, shoulders, elbows, hands, fingers. Your neck, jaw, your face, the top of your head. For each part of your body, ask yourself: do I hurt? How do I hurt? How can I be healed?

You don't need the answers here. You don't need to know anything at all. But you need to be willing to ask the question: *is this okay? Is this what I want?*

Consider your whole body; and bring your attention back to your breath, in and out. *Is this okay? Do I hurt? How can I be healed? What do I hope to heal?*

Follow the breath for a few moments more, and open your eyes: open your eyes, and consider the world around you, the world that you change every moment just by existing, and the world that changes you.

A Message from the Body

It might be helpful to you now to write down some of the discoveries you've just made: the hurts that you've suffered and the things you're hoping to heal. This is because pain, in reiki, isn't just pain: it's a message from the body. The brilliant body is as capable of communicating as the mind, but relies on cruder tools.

....
....
....
....
....
....
....
....
....
....
....
....

I want to stress at this juncture that, contrary to some perceptions of reiki, there is no insinuation here that negative thoughts are the cause of chronic illness. There is and should never be any excuse for implying that cancer, say, can be blamed on anything the patient did or said. You are not responsible for your pain – and yet perhaps there is something empowering, something important, in understanding that we are responsible for our *responses* to our own pain. We are, when all is said and done, uniquely responsible for our own happiness. And it is only when we *accept* our own responsibility for our own happiness that we can begin to make it happen.

So let's consider, then, the message that is pain. Pain is not a solid state: pain is *action*. Pain is a series of continuous nerve signals: continuous energy, sometimes misfiring.

What Does Pain Tell Us?

Pain is not so much a noun as it is a verb: *it hurts.* What hurts? Pain, in biology, is a warning. It often means we need to stop; to remove our hand from the hot plate or our tongue from the ice. It means *stop.* It means *slow down.* This is the neurological function of pain: to warn us of danger, and this is the basis of everything we're going to look at now. How is this pain warning us of danger? How might this pain be asking us to slow down? How might this pain require us to stop, and what would that stopping look like? What action should we take here? What action is required of us?

There are the obvious things, of course. Back pain, for example, is often directly related to how we sit – and how much we sit. Headaches are often correlated with too much time on a screen or too much close reading or not enough water. There are often reasons for our pain that are within our control, and it's only by a careful assessment of our pain – like the Full Body Scan starting on page 36) – that we can come to terms with that, and find the solution ourselves.

So let's take this one step further. Say we have a headache because we're spending too much time at a computer screen; we're working too hard. Is the headache the only way we can consider giving ourselves permission to step away from

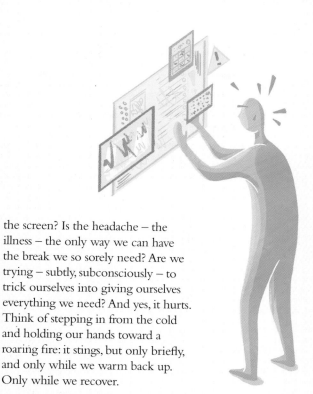

the screen? Is the headache – the illness – the only way we can have the break we so sorely need? Are we trying – subtly, subconsciously – to trick ourselves into giving ourselves everything we need? And yes, it hurts. Think of stepping in from the cold and holding our hands toward a roaring fire: it stings, but only briefly, and only while we warm back up. Only while we recover.

This makes sense, right? There are things we won't acknowledge – and things we don't even know we need.

Everything Matters

Sometimes the cause of our pain is obvious, but what about when the cause is less direct?

In reiki tradition, everything matters: everything is a metaphor. Reiki asks us to consider every possible implication of pain, and the location of pain, and see if it speaks to us in any way. We do this by thinking of all the possible words surrounding the hurt place – all the idioms, all the stories – and considering if they might have relevance for us. Might a headache imply that we are spending too much time 'in our heads' and not enough with our hearts? Might a sore throat indicate a difficulty saying what we really feel? This isn't scientific, and isn't intended to be. What it does is give us another way to tell a story about our pain. What it does is restore just a little control; it gives us back the narrative that so often – particularly in Western medicine – has been stolen from us. We are more than just bodies, more than just symptoms. We are people, and we are stories. We are verbs instead of nouns: active instead of passive.

You'll find on the opposite page an illustration of a body. Around this, I want you to jot down any words or phrases that come to mind that might help you tell a different narrative here. I've done a few to get you started.

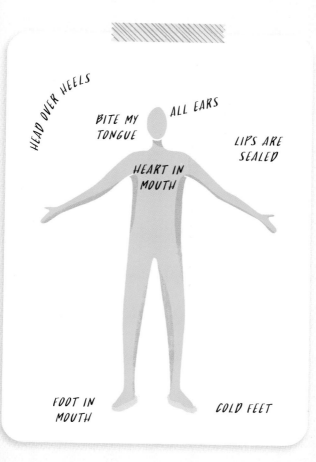

HEAD OVER HEELS

BITE MY TONGUE

ALL EARS

LIPS ARE SEALED

HEART IN MOUTH

FOOT IN MOUTH

COLD FEET

Chakras

If we understand that these metaphors can give us a new way of understanding pain, we can also go one step further: *chakras*, an ancient Sanskrit word that means 'circles'.

Now look, I understand that the word 'chakra' can feel intimidating, and indeed it's so often been co-opted by the untrained it sometimes feels that it has lost all meaning. But come with me just once more.

Do you see the seven points of light on the figure opposite? Those points of light are chakras. Each chakra relates to a certain area of the body (that which surrounds it, obviously) and each functions, basically, as a kind of focal point for our meditative energies.

We can visualize each chakra as a different colour: the seven colours of the rainbow, arranged essentially along the spine.

We can use these chakras both ways: if we have a headache, it might be that our seventh chakra is blocked because we're having trouble understanding something; conversely, if we're having trouble being understood, we might be able to heal those lines of communication by visualizing positive energy flowing through the fifth chakra (at the throat). Basically, we can use the illustration opposite both to better understand what our pain might be telling us *and* as a way of rooting our abstract problems firmly in the body.

seventh chakra: crown	violet	central nervous system	I understand
sixth chakra: third eye	indigo	eyes	I see
fifth chakra: throat	blue	ears, nose, throat	I speak, I hear
fourth chakra: heart	green	heart, lungs, chest	I love
third chakra: solar plexus	yellow	digestive system	I do
second chakra: sacral	orange	sexual organs	I feel
first chakra: root	red	spine, legs	I am

When we can visualize our pain, we can begin to understand it, and when we begin to understand it, we can begin to understand the cause. And when we understand the cause, we are one step closer to healing, whatever that healing might look like for us. In the next chapter, we'll talk a little more about the ways we can think about healing. And we'll talk, too, about the ways healing is possible for all of us.

3

Intention
The Power of the Mind

Communicating Love

Reiki lives by intention: the power of reiki comes chiefly from the intent to heal, and to be healed. We 'switch on' our reiki powers by intending to make something whole; we direct our energies by *meaning* to direct our energies.

We intend love; we give love, and when we give love often we receive love in return. Reiki can be thought of, perhaps, as a system of communicating love. And love – as we've established with the monkeys (see page 24) – has tangible health benefits. We'll get really stuck into the science of this in a minute (because it's fascinating!), but first, let's think about *intention*.

The word 'intention' has two meanings: first, and most commonly, 'a thing meant', but second, 'the healing of a wound'. That's right: in medical terms, the 'intention' of a wound is the rate of its healing. It's sometimes worth looking at the meaning of a word, and the etymology of the word, to understand the metaphors we carry with us every day. In reiki, remember, metaphors mean things: everything is intended, and nothing is by accident. There are messages for us in the everyday. There are messages within messages, and everything can help guide us gently to where we want to be. Our intentions are healing; our intentions are toward healing.

The Meaning of Intention

The word 'intention' comes from the Latin *intentio*, which has a number of meanings – tension, augmentation, exertion, charge, purpose – and which itself comes from an even older word. That word is '*intendo*', and has even *more* meanings:

I stretch out, stretch, strain	I understand
I turn my attention to	I hear
I focus	I think
I aim	I believe
I turn	I go
I direct	I travel
I intend to	I obey

Trace it back a step further: *in* + *tendo*, in Proto-Latin:

I stretch	I reach for
I stretch out	I pitch
I proceed	I speak
I strive for	

And one more step back, to Proto-Indo-European, the language from which so many more languages have sprung over thousands and thousands of years, to the root word *-ten*, which simply means:

I stretch

The intention is the stretch to the stars; our reaching out to the universe to see what reaches back for us. The intention is us speaking our truths, to strive toward something more — something greater, perhaps, than ourselves.

What do the words and phrases above bring up for you? What kind of images? Allow yourself a minute now to ponder these mental pictures, and then perhaps consider for a moment the thousands who have considered them before you, using the same words to consider the same action. As we set our own intentions, we know that we are simply the latest manifestation of energy to do so; the very words we use connect us powerfully to the past, and — indeed — to the future.

Our words are powerful. Our intentions are powerful. Our minds are stronger than we know.

The Placebo Effect

Let's take a brief diversion through something both scientifically proven and scientifically inexplicable: the placebo effect. You've almost certainly heard of this. It is the fact that sometimes our bodies can heal just as well if we merely *believe* ourselves to have been treated, rather than really taking the treatment. Your body can be 'fooled' into believing that a placebo (or 'fake') treatment is the real thing: a sugar pill that has the same effect as a painkiller, say, for curing a headache.

The word 'cure' is an interesting one – especially when we consider reiki. Can reiki 'cure' cancer? Can reiki 'cure' someone with dementia or a terminal illness? This kind of 'gotcha' gets dragged out by sceptics constantly – because, mostly, the answer seems to be no. But the sceptics are missing the point.

For a long time, it was thought that the placebo effect, as seen in scientific drug trials, simply meant that the drug being trialled was a failure. Which is, when you think about it, rather ridiculous. In what sense is consequence-free healing a failure? In what sense is it a failure to know that we have the power within our own minds to become happier and healthier?

Our minds are powerful – and let's not forget that the only reason man-made drugs work in the first place is as a kind of artificial replica of the hormones and chemicals *already present in the body.*

Bear with me here. I know this is a second leap, but I promise you it's relevant, and might just blow your mind.

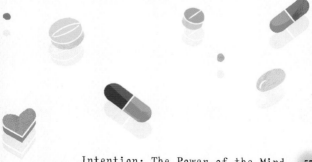

How Drugs Work

We'll get some help here from Macdonald Christie, a professor of pharmacology at The University of Sydney, Australia, who explains that drugs work kind of like a lock–and–key system.[1]

Say you have a cell. Within the cell – embedded in the membrane – are large protein molecules called receptors. These receptors receive chemical information from other, outside, molecules. Let's think of these receptors as 'the lock'.

The chemical information can come from lots of different sources outside the cell, like drugs, neurotransmitters or hormones. The molecules carrying the chemical information bind to the receptors, triggering a reaction, such as pain or pleasure. These molecules are called agonists. Let's think of these as 'keys'.

Drugs Copy What is Already Within Us

'An agonist is like the key that fits in the lock (the receptor) and turns it to open the door (or send a biochemical or electrical signal to exert an effect),' writes Christie. 'The natural agonist is the master key but it is possible to design other keys (agonist drugs) that do the same job.'

Every drug that has an effect on the human body does so *only* because it is mimicking something *already present in our own minds*. 'Morphine – or heroin that turns into morphine in the body – is an artificial agonist of the main opioid receptor,' Christie writes. 'Morphine, for instance, wasn't designed by the body but can be found naturally in opium poppies. By luck, it mimics the shape of the natural opioid agonists, the endorphins, that are natural pain relievers responsible for the "endorphin high".' Morphine is a mimic: a rough copy of something we are naturally and constantly producing anyway. In a similar fashion, cannabis mimics the hormone serotonin.

Our minds are so powerful that there are billion-dollar industries – both legal and illegal – just trying to mimic that which is already within us. The placebo effect is just another way of saying that – sometimes, and in some circumstances – the mind can provide everything we need.

What Does 'Cure' Really Mean?

Which isn't to say reiki can't necessarily shrink a tumour, or restore lost cognitive functions. It can't create the same effect, over and over, on a dozen different people under test conditions. (And, really, why should it? A dozen people, a dozen bodies, each unique and different and broken and marvellous and perfect and imperfect, and each reacting as people, not identical combinations of chemicals.) Reiki can't necessarily *cure* in the way modern science is obsessed with the idea of *cure* – but it's time to consider what that really means.

Too often, scientists have tried to cure by thinking only of the physical cause. They try to think of ways to outsmart the body and the mind with more and more drugs, many with dangerous and painful side effects. They are trying to cure – and in some senses, to help – without ever thinking of the person as anything other than a collection of symptoms, that amalgam of misfiring chemicals. The person is not a person any more. The person is a puzzle. The person is a problem.

Cast your mind back a minute: remember how we established that the mind and the body are powerfully interlinked? Remember how we established that thoughts are powerful things, and that intangible emotions could be written tangibly upon the body? Remember how we established ourselves as energies within energies, intrinsically linked holistically with the whole wide world?

Now consider a doctor treating only the symptoms of the body. Consider a doctor using hard drugs to override the pain felt in the body without ever considering the interior universe of the mind and the exterior world of the environment. Consider the way we use the word 'cure' to mean, primarily, a physical and total recovery of the body exclusively; how often, for example, we consider someone cured when they leave Intensive Care when, in reality, their journey is only just beginning. Reiki master Penelope Quest uses the example of a gangrenous leg: if you cut off the leg, the gangrene is cured, but the patient most certainly is not. The acute problem is solved, but the chronic problem is created. This is where the word 'cure' often falls down – and this is where reiki comes into its own. We need both systems: one for the immediate problem, and one for life. One that takes us in as whole people: body, mind and soul.

Everything Matters

We are more than our physical bodies, or rather, our physical bodies are more than we give them credit for. They are complicated, beautiful bundles of energy, transmitting and receiving powerful forces every second. Everything we do matters; everything we think matters; everything we touch, absorb and understand matters.

Which brings us back to the placebo effect, and a Harvard Medical School professor named Ted Kaptchuk. Kaptchuk formed a hypothesis, according to a 2018 article in *The New York Times Magazine,* that the placebo effect is, scientifically speaking, 'a biological response to an act of caring; that somehow the encounter itself calls forth healing and that the more intense and focused it is, the more healing it evokes'.[2] The placebo effect works because we intend it to work, and we believe it to work. The intention is one of care, and the intention is one of love. The intention shapes the mind, which shapes the body, which shapes the world.

So let's move toward our own intention. Let's heal that wound.

Intention Setting

Start – as by now you are very familiar with doing – by sitting comfortably. For a moment, let's just breathe together. In, out. In, out. You might like to return to that Full Body Scan we practised before (see page 36), just to ground you.

Intentions are all about grounding: about making a waypoint you can come back to throughout the day. The best intentions can be carried out in a single second and contemplated for hours, which sounds complicated, but really means that you should be able to both think about it *and* do it.

For example, if your intention is to be a better partner, you can ask yourself before each action: *am I being the best partner I can be, in this second, right now?*

You can also sit down and think carefully – perhaps in meditation – about the question: *what does it mean, longer term, to be the best partner I can be?*

This is the key to a successful intention: something that can be as big or small as you have time for.

The simplest form of intention setting is to start each day with one easy sentence. The sentence should begin:

Today I commit myself to...

And you should do this every day: as soon as you wake up, just take a moment or two to decide on your intention. Begin each day with a commitment, because it's by that commitment that we shape ourselves into the person we want to be: kind, careful, generous, a better parent, a better partner, a better friend.

In the space provided overleaf, I want us to set an intention every day for the week. In the space under each intention, I want us to record at the end of the day whether we felt it had any effect. Did we change our behaviour in any way? Were we improved by it? Were there any intentions that worked better than others?

TODAY I COMMIT MYSELF TO...

Monday:
....
....
....

Tuesday:
....
....
....

Wednesday:
....
....
....

Thursday:
....
....
....

Friday:
....
....
....

Saturday:
....
....
....

Sunday:
....
....
....

You've probably found that positive intentions – 'I will!' – work better than negative intentions – 'I'll try not to.' This makes perfect sense: think of it as talking to a child, and promising good consequences for good behaviour. Give your inner child some love (and useful boundaries, a sense of humour and forgiveness).

Positive affirmations give us something to stretch up to – to reach for. Think of those many definitions of intention on pages 54 and 55: none of them is about making the world smaller. None of them is about no. They are all about yes. Which brings us to our next chapter: the power of affirmation.

4

Affirmation
The Power of Yes

An affirmation is a kind of intention, and indeed the two are closely linked: we can affirm our intentions, and intend our affirmations. Our intentions will feed into our affirmations; and the more strongly we believe our affirmations the more likely we are to carry through those intentions for which we are striving.

Remember everything we've talked about? Remember the power of the mind? By speaking of ourselves in the positive, we become more positive. We allow ourselves to feel what it would be like to be the person we want to be: the person we know we *can* be. Studies have shown that positive affirmations can help everything from our practical problem-solving to our self-esteem.[3][4]

Affirmation Meditation

As ever, sit comfortably and get easy with your breath.
Give yourself a minute. Breathe out the stresses of the
world; breathe in the deepest, longest breath you've
taken all day. Breathe out that traffic jam, your
squabbling kids, the annoying email, the electricity bill.
Breathe it all out. Give yourself time.

Now, in this moment: who do you want to be?
Think of those intentions we've been setting for the
past week. Who are you in your dreams? Who would
your best self be? In the space opposite, jot down some
words. I don't want you to worry that these words are
fancy, or overblown or grandiose. I don't want you to
feel that you're asking too much. You're asking for just
the right amount.

What are your best qualities? How can you use those
qualities to be the kind of person you most want to
be? There are a few examples listed opposite and space
to write some of your own.

STRONG

CAPABLE

BRAVE

INDEPENDENT

CURIOUS

KIND

QUESTIONING

GENEROUS

SMART

And here's the thing: you already are everything you just wrote down. I swear to you. All those ideas — all those big dreams — are in your mind already, and you can achieve them, and you can manifest them. Remember right at the beginning of this book when I told you you were already enough? There's space for all of you here, and space for all the things we both know you can be.

I want you to pick your favourite word you wrote down. And now I want you to say it aloud. Just the word. Say it again. Say it again. Say it louder this time. Say it louder! Say it louder! Keep saying it! Say it until you feel silly, say it until you really feel it!

Now we're going to go a step further: say, 'I am' and then your word. I am brave. I am kind. I am strong. I am strong! Say it with an exclamation mark. Say it until you're smiling. I am brave! I am kind! I am strong! Say it again. Say it until you're sick of it. Say it until you're mad at me for asking you to say it again and again and again.

One more step: say, 'I, [your name], am' and then your word. I know how silly you feel! But I want you to keep doing it! I want you to keep saying it! And here's the thing: I want you to say it every single day. I want you to say it every time you look in a mirror. I want you to say it until you believe it – and we know by now how strong the power of belief can be. And I believe in you.

Fake it 'Til You Make it

A positive affirmation helps us to overcome particular negative ideas we have already about our own bodies: essentially, it's *fake it 'til you make it*. While this has been folk wisdom for hundreds of years, it's actually backed up by science. Studies have shown that faking positivity really can make you happy: scholars at the University of Tennessee in the USA in 2019 collated over 130 different research projects, consisting of more than 11,000 participants, and found 'smiling makes people feel happier, scowling makes them feel angrier, and frowning makes them feel sadder'.[5] The energy we project into the world is the energy we get in return: *what you give is what you get*.

You get out what you put in.

Reiki master Penelope Quest tells us that this – along with 'what you resist, persists' – is at the heart of reiki.

We are part of a vast web of energy, and everything is connected. This doesn't mean — just as was explained in the last chapter — that bad things happen because you somehow deserved them. It simply means that the way you handle bad things will make a huge difference to how you perceive them. It's about facing what the world gives you as the kind of person you want to be, and — once again — telling the kind of story you want to live.

Finding Greater Joys in Small Joys

A positive mental attitude, popularly called by the acronym PMA, is defined as 'finding greater joys in small joys', and the development of this way of living is crucial to living the kind of life you like. There have even been studies that show PMA can help us overcome physical problems like cancer – which is, of course, not to say that people who don't survive are in any way at fault.[6] Rather, what it tells us is that PMA can be enormously helpful in the ongoing treatment, recovery and acceptance of things that – so far – Western science has not managed to solve. Patients undergoing reiki often report requiring less pain medication and that they feel less stressed – and as we know, stress is a major reason for ill health in the first place!

You see, PMA has in the last century come to form the backbone of the branch of psychology known as positive psychology. This branch sets itself up in opposition to the 'mental-illness' model of thinking, and is concerned not with tragedy and pain, but with hope, optimism and wellness. This is how we have to look at pain from a reiki perspective,

and from the perspective of this book: not as a punishment, not as a negative, but as a helpful, useful tool in furthering our understanding of ourselves. Pain is information that can help us, and when we consider healing from that perspective, things start to become a little easier to understand.

Gratitude Makes Everything Better

Intention and affirmation reduce our stress; taking the time for meditation and reiki allows us to communicate with our bodies in new ways. By contemplating the holistic approach we are finally free from the burden of thinking of ourselves as problems rather than people. We are free to choose happiness. We are free to be glad for what we have, instead of regretting that which we lack. We are free to be grateful.

Gratitude is scientifically proven to make everything better. No, I'm serious. Gratitude makes everything better, even terrible situations. They have run studies using this thing called a Gratitude Journal – and we're about to make one for ourselves, too! – that show that the positive mood of the subjects increases dramatically when they use a Gratitude Journal. They report that they are happier with everything in their lives: their homes, their careers, their families and, most of all, themselves. Gratitude increases empathy, which increases bonding: it connects us to our people, and them to us. It grounds us in the world in which we belong, which helps us stay healthy, happy and whole.

Less Negativity Equals Better Mental Wellness

A study conducted at the University of California, Berkeley asked nearly three hundred people to participate in research into this subject.[7] 'Participants were randomly assigned to one of three conditions: (a) control (psychotherapy only), (b) a psychotherapy plus expressive writing, and (c) a psychotherapy plus gratitude writing,' the study tells us. Basically: some people just got therapy; some people got therapy and wrote about their feelings; and the third group got therapy and wrote letters – every single day! – expressing their gratitude to someone or something in their life.

The grateful participants reported significantly improved mental health on an ongoing basis. They also, incidentally, reported better sleep and less pain. The act of gratitude healed them. The act of being grateful for what they did have made them less aware of what they lacked.

We have to *want* what we *have* – not just strive to *have* what we *want*.

It's interesting to note that in this study, the Berkeley scientists drew special attention to the fact that the grateful participants 'used a higher percentage of positive emotion words and "we" words, and a lower proportion of negative emotion words'. The lack of negativity was specifically marked as a reason for their ongoing mental wellness and had lasting effects on the brain. In fact, it made them more able to recognize gratitude – and happiness – in their futures, too. The more we practise happiness, the more happy we become.

You can train yourself to be happy. You can train yourself to be grateful. So let's start right now.

EXERCISE:

Gratitude Journal

The act of writing changes you. This is scientifically proven, time and time again: when we write about our feelings – and in particular our positive feelings – we simply *feel better*. So we're going to write. We need the physical record of writing for this to work.

While there's some space opposite for you to write in, you'll probably want to grab a new notebook (and a nice pen!) for this exercise. There's something lovely about taking a new notebook – about choosing something just for you – that seems to fit with the tone of the exercise, don't you think?

This notebook is now your Gratitude Journal, and you're going to write in it once a week for the foreseeable future. Just once a week (although feel free to jot down any extra gratitudes you really want to remember), because this is what's most effective for actually stimulating lasting change. Once a week, you'll take *15 minutes to write down 5 things you've been grateful for this week*.

Five things I've been grateful for this week:

1 ....
....

2 ....
....

3 ....
....

4 ....
....

5 ....
....

Don't phone this in! According to Robert A Emmons, the world's leading gratitude expert, we have to *want* to become happy. (Which makes sense, given everything we've learned so far about the mind and the body.) You have to commit to this: put your hand on your heart (yes, I know you feel silly) and breathe. Breathe out the toxic negativity; breathe in gratitude. Breathe in love. Be grateful, if you can, for the fact you're able to breathe, and breathe clean air, and take this time. A huge part of gratitude therapy is the slow understanding that everything is a gift: the air, the time, the space.

Emmons told the Berkeley researchers that their subjects should be 'aware of the depth of their gratitude', and you should take the time to really work out what exactly it is you're grateful for. Be specific: you're not just grateful for your friends, but for the fact that Lorelei called you just to say hi or the fact that Cassius made a fuss of your birthday or the fact that

Danielle always remembers that you hate cheese on your pizza. You're not just grateful for your kid, but for the adorable way she tells you she loves you or the fact she went to bed with a little less fuss than the night before. You're not just grateful for your home, but for the way your favourite chair supports your back. Specificity helps gratitude immensely.

On the following pages, you'll find some prompts to help you if you get stuck…

- An old relationship that helped form me into who I am

- A new relationship that excites me

- Someone who inspires me

- A stranger who made a difference to me

- An interaction that simply made me smile

- One thing I like about my appearance today

- One thing I like about my mind

- What am I really, really good at?

- What opportunity do I have today that others maybe don't have?

- What one, nearby object do I love? It could be a perfectly weighted coffee cup, a pen that writes smoothly, a picture on the wall that makes me smile!

- What place do I love? Why do I love it? When did I last go? How lucky am I to have seen this place and been there at all!

- Did I eat anything delicious? Did I have a perfect cup of tea?

- Did I see anything beautiful? Sunlight on a puddle? The face of my kid? The perfect shade of lipstick?

- Did I hear anything good? A voice, a song, a secret?

The trick, as in every chapter of this book, is to start to notice the world you live in: to understand that we are a part of it, and it is a part of us. We are formed of our experiences, and of our senses, physically as well as mentally.

We belong to the world and it, in turn, belongs to us. We are connected to everything around us, and it is this, more than anything else, that gives reiki its power.

Epilogue

Connection:
The Power of Love

Reiki works, as you know, by a system of hands on the body. We move our attuned hands, full of the intention to heal, across the body of the patient; we push our good energy into theirs, and we move their energy along with ours.

We improve the flow; we change; we translate our positivity into their positivity, and help them understand their pain. We understand their pain, and we touch; we touch in a way that is tender and loving. We take our time to touch. We take our time to understand. We listen to the body, and we listen to the mind, and we listen (difficult word coming up…) to the soul.

The Soul is Everything

We have not talked so much directly about the soul in this book, because it's such a huge concept that this *Little Book* can't really touch it. It means so many things to so many people. It's so overwhelming; it's everything; it's subjective and nebulous and often thinking about it makes people rather worried. The mind we understand; the body we understand; but the soul? That can feel a bit daunting.

And yet, of course, it's at the heart of everything. It's at the heart of everything we've been doing.

Let's look at it like this: the soul is the manifestation of the energy within us that goes when we go. The soul is the spirit; it is the energy that flows through the living body, which powers the mind and moves the body.

In India, the traditional greeting is *namaste*; in colloquial terms, it simply means 'hello', but the real meaning goes much deeper. *Nama* means 'to bow' or 'to bend', and it comes from two Sanskrit words: *na*, which means 'not', and *ma*, which means 'mine'. Not mine, but the eternal. Not mine, but the divine. *Te* means 'you'; and all this, too, is a metaphor. When taken together, the whole means something like 'the spirit in me greets the spirit in you.'

Press your palms together; incline the head. *Namaste.*
The spirit in me greets the spirit in you.

This is how we can think of the soul – that which we have been nourishing, teaching, understanding over the course of this book: the spirit, the not-mine, the eternal. The energy that flows through me, and into you; the energy that makes us part of the vast shimmering universe all around us; the energy that we transfer through the system of reiki.

And yet it is, as I have said, impossible to teach the principles of reiki via a book. So what now? If I haven't taught you how to heal, then what has been the point of this book?

Connection

The point, as always, is *connection*. It is to give to others that which we have freed up in ourselves: positive energy, positive flow, gratitude. We know that our thoughts can influence our physical being; we know that our actions affect the actions of others; we know that actions influence thoughts, influence feelings, influence thoughts, influence actions. Everything is connected, and everything we do matters.

When we feel good, we make others feel good, and that in itself is healing. That in itself is powerful magic. We learn first to love ourselves and we send that love out into the universe. Breathe love in, and breathe love out. We intend love; we give love; we communicate love; and so we change the world. As simple as that.

Love:

Our *mysterious atmosphere*

Our *miraculous sign*

The *universal energy*

Notes

1   Christie, Macdonald. 'Explainer: how do drugs work?' The
    Conversation. theconversation.com/explainer-how-do-drugs-
    work-48665, accessed 19 October 2020.

2   Greenberg, Gary. 'What if the Placebo Effect Isn't A Trick?' *The New
    York Times Magazine* (2018). www.nytimes.com/2018/11/07/
    magazine/placebo-effect-medicine.html, accessed 19 October 2020.

3   Creswell J D, Dutcher J M, Klein W M P, Harris P R, Levine J M.
    'Self-Affirmation Improves Problem-Solving Under Stress'. 2013; *PLOS
    ONE* 8(5): e62593. https://doi.org/10.1371/journal.pone.0062593,
    accessed 22 October 2020.

4   Peden A R, Rayens M K, Hall L A, Beebe L H. 'Preventing Depression
    in High-Risk College Women: A Report of an 18-Month Follow-Up'.
    2001; *Journal of American College Health* 49(6): 299–306.
    doi:10.1080/07448480109596316, accessed 22 October 2020.

5   University of Tennessee at Knoxville. 'Psychologists Find Smiling Really
    Can Make People Happier.' ScienceDaily (2019). www.sciencedaily.
    com/releases/2019/04/190412094728.htm, accessed 19 October 2020.

6   Rom S A, Miller L, Peluso J. 'Playing the Game: Psychological Factors in
    Surviving Cancer'. 2009; *International Journal of Emergency Mental Health
    and Human Resilience* 11(1): 25–35.

7   Wong Y J, Owen J, Gabana N T, Brown J W, McInnis S, Toth P and
    Gilman L. 'Does Gratitude Writing Improve the Mental Health of
    Psychotherapy Clients? Evidence from a Randomized Controlled Trial'.
    2018; *Psychotherapy Research* 28(2): 192–202.